FOLGER M⸙⸙⸙⸙⸙⸙⸙⸙⸙⸙⸙⸙⸙⸙⸙⸙⸙⸙OL

P9-BYT-910

★ IT'S MY STATE! ★
Texas

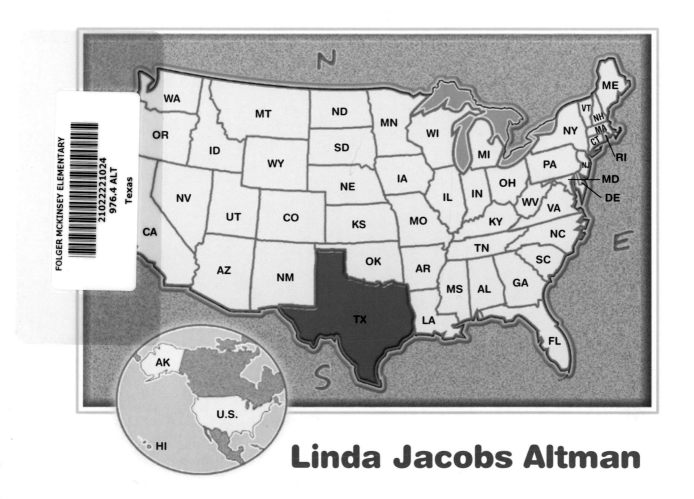

FOLGER MCKINSEY ELEMENTARY

976.4 ALT

Texas

21022221024

Linda Jacobs Altman

BENCHMARK BOOKS

MARSHALL CAVENDISH
NEW YORK

Series Consultant

David G. Vanderstel, Ph.D., Executive Director, National Council on Public History

With thanks to Cynthia Brandimarte, Ph.D., Senior Advisor for Historic Sites, State Parks Division, Texas Parks and Wildlife Department, for her expert review of this manuscript

Benchmark Books
Marshall Cavendish
99 White Plains Road
Tarrytown, New York 10591-9001
www.marshallcavendish.com

Text, maps, and illustrations copyright © 2003 by Marshall Cavendish Corporation
Maps and illustrations by Christopher Santoro

All rights reserved. No part of this book may be reproduced or utilized in any form or by any means electronic or mechanical including photocopying, recording, or by any information storage and retrieval system, without permission from the copyright holders.

Library of Congress Cataloging-in-Publication Data

Altman, Linda Jacobs, 1943-
Texas / by Linda Jacobs Altman.
p. cm. — (It's my state!)
Summary: Surveys the history, geography, government, and economy of the
Lone Star State as well as the diverse ways of life of its people.
Includes bibliographical references and index.
ISBN 0-7614-1423-1
1. Texas—Juvenile literature. [1. Texas.] I. Title. II.
Series.
F386.3 .A66 2002
976.4—dc21
2002002709

Photo research by Candlepants, Inc.

Cover Photo: *Bob Daemmrich Photo, Inc.*

Back cover illustration: The license plate shows Texas's postal abbreviation, followed by its year of statehood.

The photographs in this book are used by permission and through the courtesy of: *Corbis:* Wolfgang Kaehler, 4 (top); Raymond Gehman, 4 (bottom); David Muench, 5 (top), 8, 9, 14, 21 (middle), 71 (middle); Michelle Garrett, 5 (middle); James L. Amos, 5 (bottom); D. Boone, 11; Tom Bean, 13; Philip Gould, 15; Mary Ann McDonald, 20 (middle); Joe McDonald, 20 (bottom); Scott T. Smith, 21 (top); Darrell Gulin, 21 (bottom); Roger Ressmeyer, 37 (bottom); James A. Sugar, 41; Bettmann, 46 (top), 47 (top); Corbis, 46 (middle); Wally McNamee, 46 (bottom); Sygma / Austin American Statesman, 47 (middle); Douglas Kirkland, 47 (bottom); George H.H. Huey, 56; Kit Kittle, 67; Craig Aurness, 68; Morton Beebe, 70 (top); Joe McDonald, 70 (middle); Richard Hamilton Smith, 70 (bottom); Julie Habel; 71 (top); Lowell Georgia, 71 (bottom); Fukuhara, Inc., 72; Mark L. Stephenson, 75; Tom Bean, 75. *AnimalsAnimals:* David Welling, 4 (middle); J&P Wegner, 18; Zig Leszcynski, 19; E.R. Degginger, 20 (top). *Bob Daemmrich Photo Inc.:* 17, 38, 40, 44, 48, 50, 51, 52, 54, 55, 59, 61, 62, 64, 66. *Amon Carter Museum, Fort Worth, Texas, Gift of Mr. And Mrs. Allan M. Disman (detail):* 22. *The Bridgman Art Library, Private Collection:* 24. *The Witte Museum San Antonio, Texas:* 25. *Tulane University Library:* 27. *Center for American History, UT-Austin:* ct#0008/Prints and Photographs Collection, 28; cn#02855 oral History of Texas Oil Pioneers, 34. *James Perry Bryan Collection:* 28. *Texas State Library and Archives Commission:* 29. *State Preservation Board of Texas:* 30; *Courtesy of Larry Sheerin:* 31. *The UT Institute of Texan Cultures at San Antonio no. 73-817 / Courtesy of Texas Southmost College Library:* 33. *Tyrrell Historical Society:* 36. *DeShields Collection, Daughters of the Republic of Texas Library, cn96.102:* 37 (top).

Book design by Anahid Hamparian

Printed in Italy

1   3   5   6   4   2

Contents

A Quick Look at Texas

Nickname: The Lone Star State

Population: 20,851,820 (2000)

Statehood: 1845

Flower: Bluebonnet

Bluebonnets once grew wild on the prairies. Today, they grow along highways, planted there by the Texas Department of Transportation. Texans love this little flower. The bluebonnet has its own song, its own festival, and even its own town: Ennis, the Bluebonnet City of Texas.

Bird: Mockingbird

Mockingbirds are natural mimics. They can imitate the songs and sounds of other birds. They are also uncommonly brave. Nesting mockingbirds have been known to swoop down on dogs, cats, and even human beings who "invade" their territory.

Tree: Pecan

According to Texas legend, the pecan was chosen in honor of James Stephen Hogg, the first native-born governor of Texas. When Hogg died in 1906, he left a strange last request; he wanted a pecan tree planted on his grave. This was done, and in 1919 the pecan became the official state tree.

Plant: Prickly Pear Cactus

The prickly pear is the most common cactus in Texas. It has flat pear-shaped pads that hold water. The prickly pear is a regular in many Texas kitchens. Its fruit can be peeled and tossed into salads or served alone as a vegetable, and it makes a delicious jelly.

Dish: Chili

No dish says "Texas" more than a steaming hot bowl of chili. The state even has an organization called the Chili Appreciation Society. Each year, it hosts a world championship chili cook-off in the town of Terlingua. Texan cooks come from all around to compete with their best recipes.

Folk Dance: Square Dance

This lively dance features a "square" of couples performing patterned steps. A caller sings out the steps in time to the music. Dancers must learn how to do patterns with names like allemande, sashay, and promenade. Square-dance clubs all over the state offer classes for beginners and hold competitions for experienced dancers.

TEXAS

Amarillo

Palo Duro
Canyon

El Paso

Dallas

Austin

Houston

San
Marcos
Aquarena
Center

Johnson
Space
Center

Big Bend
National Park

San
Antonio

Rio Grande River

N
W E
S

0   100 Miles

1 The Lone Star State

Texas is the second-largest American state after Alaska. It covers about 266,807 square miles of the south-central United States. Within this vast territory are many landforms, from the beaches and marshlands of the Gulf coast to the sagebrush and cactus of the southwestern desert. In between are hills and canyons, wide grassland prairies, and forests thick with trees.

Texas is usually divided into four geographic areas: the arid mountains and basins region in the far west, the Great Plains in the northwest and north-central part of the state, the central lowlands in the middle, and the Gulf coastal plain in the east and southeast. These main areas are in turn divided into subregions.

Texas Borders
North: Oklahoma and Arkansas
South: Mexico
East: Arkansas, Louisiana, and the Gulf of Mexico
West: New Mexico

West Texas

The mountains and basins region is also called the Big Bend country. A large loop, or bend, in the Rio Grande ("big river" in Spanish) forms the southern border and separates Texas from Mexico.

It is a place of windblown basins, or lowlands, and craggy mountain ranges. Distances are vast and water is in short supply. The area

Guadalupe Peak in the Big Bend country rises to 8,749 feet. It is the highest mountain in Texas.

averages only twelve inches of rainfall a year. Plants, animals, and even people must adapt to the dry conditions in order to survive. Mostly because of the lack of water, the Big Bend country has very few people. Its only large city is El Paso, with 606,526 people.

The Rio Grande forms a natural border between Texas and Mexico. It is slow moving and muddy in most places.

A storm rolling in over the wide-open spaces of the Texas plains is an impressive sight.

Northeast of the Big Bend country lies the high plains region of the Texas Panhandle. This dry plateau (raised flat land) is split in the north by the Canadian River. Stiff winds sweep across the prairie, raising clouds of sand. Sudden downpours turn dry riverbeds into channels for flash floods. Storms called blue northers bring freezing winds from the Rocky Mountains.

The Panhandle is cattle country. Herds of beef cattle graze the short, tough buffalo grass that covers the prairie. Though the region is roughly the size of West Virginia, its total population is only about 400,000. Of that number, about 350,000 live in the two biggest cities of Amarillo and Lubbock. The rest are spread among ranches and tiny country towns. Some of these towns are so small they have no newspapers or grocery stores.

Only fifty people live in the Panhandle town of Mentone. A favorite local pastime is making up tourist slogans for the town. One favorite is:

We're not in the middle of nowhere, but you can see it from here.

Central Texas

The Caprock Escarpment is a steep cliff on the eastern edge of the Panhandle plateau. It separates the high plains of the Panhandle from the lower central plains. The northern part of this region is often called the rolling plains because of its gentle hills. Like the Panhandle, it is part of the Great Plains of the American Midwest. This vast area was once tall grass prairie. Herds of buffalo thundered across these lands, grazing on the thick tall grasses.

Today, the buffalo are gone and so is the tall grass. The region is the most populated in Texas, with most people clustered in the Dallas-Fort Worth area.

South of the rolling plains is the Edwards plateau, or hill country. The terrain is rugged, but not particularly high; three thousand feet is the top elevation. This is the heart of Texas, dotted with rivers, streams, and lakes and known for its beauty. Austin, the capital of the state and its largest city, is here.

In 1934, Dallas city promoters
put up a huge neon Pegasus, or flying horse,
on the tallest building in town.
Then they put an identical Pegasus on the other side.
The reason? They didn't want anybody calling
Dallas a one-horse town.

Dallas at sunset is a dramatic sight. The city's skyline is one of the most famous in Texas.

The Balcones Canyonlands is one of the most dramatic subregions. It has cliff faces so steep they seem like walls, and exposed rock formations that were ancient long before human beings came to Texas.

East Texas

The coastal plain of east Texas is the largest natural region in the state. The northwestern part of the region is heavily forested with oak and other hardwoods. These forests alternate with blackland prairies, where the soil is dark and rich. Locals call this soil black gumbo after the thick, stewlike dish that is a Texas favorite.

East along the Louisiana border, oaks and other hardwoods give way to pine trees. The piney woods, as it is known, is part of a vast and ancient pine forest that once covered much of the Southeast. It was once dense and dark and undisturbed. Even today, few people live in the piney woods. There are more farms, ranches, and lumbering operations than cities and suburbs. Its largest city is Tyler, with about 80,000 people.

South of the piney woods, the Texas coastline follows the Gulf of Mexico. The Gulf coast is a place of sandy beaches and wetlands, or marshes, teeming with life. The majestic whooping crane winters here. Sea turtles swim in the coastal waters.

In the 1980s, ridley sea turtles were nearly extinct. But people in Mexico and Texas worked together and protected the eggs in their nests. After the eggs hatched, the babies were carried gently to the Gulf! Today, the ridleys have a fighting chance to survive.

The endangered whooping crane has found a home in a Gulf coast wildlife refuge. Here, the birds and their habitat are protected.

The Lone Star State

The prickly pear cactus is a showy symbol of Texas. The red flowers are called claret cup.

Alligators prowl the marshlands, occasionally coming into contact with human beings. Game wardens at the Texas Parks and Wildlife Department get fifty or sixty frantic "alligator calls" a year. Somebody has usually run over an alligator on the highway or found one in their backyard. "People think they're rare, but they're not," said game warden Danny Kelso. "There's an endless supply of 'gators." When possible, game wardens trap the animals and release them into a wildlife preserve.

Inland from the Gulf, the Rio Grande valley is the southern-most tip of the coastal plain. The valley is a lowland desert, with mesquite trees, prickly pear cactuses, and rootless tumbleweeds scurrying ahead of the wind. With irrigation (a manmade watering system), the valley's soil is fertile. Its farms produce a variety of fruits and vegetables, including spinach, peanuts, and strawberries.

Rich Texas farmland, ready for planting.

Climate

Joking about the climate is a Texas tradition. Texans have been known to say that their state has four seasons: drought, flood, blizzard, and twister. Like most humor, this has a grain of truth. All these extremes can happen in Texas.

West Texas is the coldest part of the state, with an average annual temperature of 54 degrees Fahrenheit. Summer days are fiercely hot, but temperatures plunge at night. Even in July and August, west Texans often grab a sweater after sunset. Winter brings blizzards that blanket the prairie in snow.

The hottest part of Texas is the Rio Grande valley, known for mild winters and crackling hot summers. The Gulf coast escapes the hot summers because of the marine, or ocean, air from the Gulf of Mexico. Winters are equally mild, with never a trace of snow. But this almost ideal climate can be spoiled by fierce storms coming from the Gulf. These storms can be deadly. The Galveston hurricane of 1900 is considered the worst natural disaster in American history. It destroyed the city and killed over six thousand people.

It's so hot the hens are layin' hard boiled eggs.
— Heard in Texas on a sweltering summer day

Wildlife

Like the climate and the land, Texas wildlife varies by region. It ranges from rattlesnakes and roadrunners in the western desert to beavers, raccoons, and white-tailed deer in the eastern woodlands.

The Rio Grande valley has some of the most unusual species. Tropical creatures like the ocelot and the coatimundi

Children play on the beach of Padre Island, Texas.

The Lone Star State

(kuh-wat-tee-MUHN-dee) have migrated north from Mexico. The coatimundi, or coati for short, is related to the raccoon, with a longer face and tail. It looks for food in trees as well as on the ground, living mainly on insects.

The ocelot is a cat about twice the size of an ordinary house cat. It lives in the brush country of southern Texas, hunting birds, rabbits, and small rodents. The most striking feature of the ocelot is its beautiful spotted fur. For many years, it was hunted for that fur. Its habitat shrunk as dense

The coatimundi may look cute, but it is not a pet. It has strong claws and knows how to use them.

The wild beauty of the ocelot makes it a favorite with animal watchers at zoos and wildlife sanctuaries.

brush was cleared for farmland. Today, the ocelot is on the endangered species list. Residents of the southern Rio Grande valley are working to save this beautiful cat. They are restoring its habitat by planting native shrubs in dense areas.

Prehistoric pterosaurs once glided through the skies of south Texas. They were reptiles, not birds. The largest of them had a fifty-foot wingspan and weighed nearly two hundred pounds.

Even in these days of disappearing wildlife habitat and fast-growing cities, Texas is still known for its "wide open spaces." Modern Texans like things that way. They may be more likely to drive the highways than ride horses on the range, but they still treasure the land as an important part of their heritage.

Plants & Animals

Armadillo

No animal is more associated with Texas than the armadillo. This little roly-poly creature is about the size of a cat and has a bony, scaly shell on its back to protect it from predators. The armadillo eats insects and occasionally snakes and lives in burrows that it digs in the ground. It can be found in every part of Texas except the western desert.

Horned Lizard

This little "horny toad" has hornlike spikes. Short-legged and very slow, it lives on a diet of red ants, often following ant trails and eating as it goes. Horned lizards were once so abundant that the legislature made them the state reptile. Today they are rare, but a group called the Texas Horned Lizard Conservation Society is working to save the lizards and their habitat.

Roadrunner

This long, loosely built bird made famous by a cartoon can often be seen racing across the sands of west Texas. When it cries "beep, beep," it sounds a bit like a honking horn. The roadrunner lives on a diet of insects and small reptiles.

Cactus

Many kinds of cactuses can be found in the deserts of Texas. Their thick fleshy stems act as a water-storage system. Because of this, cactuses have saved many lives. People lost without water can cut off a piece of some types of cactus and suck moisture from the pulp.

Mesquite

With its crooked limbs growing close to the ground, mesquite has a "bushy" appearance. But it can grow tall enough to be called a tree. In dry climates, mesquite survives because a large and deep root system makes good use of available water.

Wildflowers

Texas has about four thousand species of wildflowers. From the dainty bluebonnet to the majestic sunflower, they grow in many colors and shapes. Wildflowers on a Texas prairie in springtime are quite a sight!

2 From the Beginning

Texas has been part of six different countries: Spain, France, Mexico, the Texas Republic, the United States, and the Confederacy. Texas's written history begins with the Spanish explorers of the sixteenth century. Its unwritten history goes back much farther.

Long before European explorers arrived, Native American tribes lived in all parts of what is now Texas. The early tribes included the Caddo in east Texas; the Atakapa and Karankawa along the coast; and the Tonkawa, Tigua, and Kickapoo in the west.

> The Caddo people of east Texas helped to name the state. Texas comes from their word for friend.

The First Flag: Spain, 1519-1821

Spanish interest in Texas began as early as 1519, when a sea captain named Alonzo Alvarez de Pineda mapped the Gulf coastline. The next explorers had heard legends of golden cities, in which fabulous wealth was there for the taking. They found only an untamed and beautiful land occupied by people who cared nothing for gold.

Boys, called newsies, sell newspapers in Beaumont, Texas, in 1913.

Around 1540, Francisco Vásquez de Coronado searched for "El Dorado"—the city of gold. He found only the endless, arid plains of Texas.

In 1682, the first permanent settlement was established near present-day El Paso. As the Spanish claimed and settled lands, they came into conflict with the people who already lived there. The idea that anyone could own the land was strange to Native Americans. They knew nothing of deeds, land grants, and property rights. The land belonged to no one; therefore, it belonged to everyone. But the Europeans kept coming. And eventually the Native Americans lost their land and their way of life.

Some tribes were conquered, forced to practice Christianity, and made to work for the Spanish missions. The missions were not just churches. They were complete settlements. The main complex was usually surrounded by a wall. Inside were workshops, supply rooms, and living quarters as well as the church. The complex was surrounded by planted fields and pastureland. The Native American converts lived at the mission and worked long, hard hours in the fields. They did not get paid for this work, nor were they allowed to leave.

The Spanish introduced the horse to the native peoples of America. Tribes like the Apache and Comanche became skilled riders.

The tribes that escaped this fate lived by raiding Spanish settlements. For as long as the Spanish flag flew over Texas, settlers were locked in an often-bloody struggle with the people they meant to displace.

A Comanche war party on the Texas plains, by artist Theodore Gentilz.

The Second Flag: France, 1685-1763

In 1685, King Louis XVI of France gave the explorer René Robert Cavelier, Sieur de La Salle four ships and a royal command: La Salle was to set up a fort at the mouth of the Mississippi River in what is now Louisiana. Because of a navigational error, La Salle landed in east Texas rather than southern Louisiana.

He decided to make the best of the situation and built the fort in Texas. The result was Fort St. Louis, named in honor of the king. It was a wooden stockade surrounded by seven log cabins.

La Salle soon realized that he had chosen a bad location. Fort St. Louis was built on marshland in the heart of Karankawa country. The Karankawa were a warlike people who did not take kindly to strangers in their midst. They captured or killed many unwary French people. The settlement lasted only a few years. In 1687, La Salle was killed during a mutiny of his men. Sometime later, Karankawa warriors overran the fort he had built.

Other French people continued to settle on the Gulf coast of Louisiana and Texas. Their colonies thrived until 1763, when France lost its American possessions to England. The British claimed all French territories east of the Mississippi, except for New Orleans. Texas remained in Spanish hands.

The Third Flag: Mexico, 1821-1836

In 1821, Mexico won independence from Spain, and a new flag flew over Texas: the eagle banner of the Mexican nation. The new government was not very interested in Texas. An

In the early 1800s, French settlers from Louisiana developed an interest in Texas. They established several colonies in the eastern part of the state.

Stephen F. Austin established the first American colony in Texas. Because of this, he is known as "the father of Texas."

American named Stephen F. Austin *was* interested. He asked for and won permission to start an American colony in the northeast. In return for land, he agreed that the settlers would become citizens of Mexico and obey its laws. Austin himself kept this agreement. He even changed his first name to the Spanish Estévan. Austin was strict about the type of settlers he would allow in his colony. He said, "[N]o frontiersman who has no other occupation than that of hunter will be received—no drunkard, no gambler, no profane swearer, no idler."

Many other settlers did not take their Mexican citizenship seriously. They were Mexican citizens in name only. They did not understand the culture or the language, nor were they interested in learning. It was only a matter of time before conflict between these two very different cultures erupted into a full-scale war.

On March 2, 1836, Texas declared independence from Mexico. While Texan leaders met at Washington-on-the-Brazos (the Brazos is a river in Texas), Mexican troops were already besieging the Alamo. For twelve days, a force of 150 men held off an army of thousands. Their stand bought precious time for the Texans to organize their forces.

The last stand at the Alamo, by artist Henry Arthur McArdle.

On April 21, 1836, Sam Houston led a ragtag army of Texans against Mexican forces at San Jacinto. Houston was the perfect choice to command a small force of irregulars against a much larger force of professional soldiers. He knew how to inspire his men as well as how to plan a battle. In a short, fierce battle, they won the day. Sam Houston became a Texas hero, and Texas became an independent republic.

Sam Houston and his men defeated a superior Mexican force in the Battle of San Jacinto. Painting by Henry Arthur McArdle.

The Fourth Flag: The Republic of Texas, 1836–1845

The now-famous Lone Star banner of Texas became the flag of the new republic. Sam Houston became its first president and Stephen F. Austin, its secretary of state.

I have traveled near five hundred miles across Texas, and am now enabled to judge pretty near correctly of the soil, and the resources of the Country, and I have no hesitancy to pronouncing it the finest country . . . upon the globe.

— Sam Houston

Texas was not ready to become a nation. It had no monetary system, no national capital, and no standing army to defend its citizens. In the south, Mexico continued to be a threat, even though there was no formal declaration of war. In the west, Native American tribes continued to raid settlements and tried to drive the Texans off the land.

In 1844, Texas petitioned the United States government for statehood. On December 29, 1845, it became the twenty-eighth state to enter the Union.

A surveying party works in Texas during the days of the Republic.

The Fifth Flag: The United States, 1845–1861 and 1870–Present

When Texas became a state, U.S. President James Polk wanted to secure its southern border at the Rio Grande. He also wanted to bring California and New Mexico into the nation. At the time, "New Mexico" was bigger than the present state with that name. It included the entire American Southwest between Texas and California.

Polk offered to buy Mexican claims in the region. Mexico refused to sell. It also renounced its treaties with Texas and renewed its claims to the territory. The president responded by sending American troops to Texas.

General Zachary Taylor, who led the first battle of the Mexican War, would become the twelfth president of the United States in 1849.

The first battle of the Mexican War was fought on Texas soil on May 8, 1846. General Zachary Taylor sent word to President Polk that the fighting had begun. Five days later, the United States declared war on Mexico.

The war ended two years after it began. The United States and Mexico signed the Treaty of Guadalupe Hidalgo on February 2, 1848. Mexico was forced to give up—or cede—Texas, New Mexico, and California to the United States in exchange for $15 million.

The end of the war did not stop border fights in the Rio Grande valley or Indian raids in the west. South and west Texas remained dangerous places for settlers to live. East Texas, however, was relatively peaceful. It became a vast cotton-growing area owned by white "gentlemen farmers" and worked by black slaves.

The Sixth Flag: The Confederacy, 1861–1865

When the Civil War began in 1861, Texas withdrew from the Union and joined the Confederate States of America. Many Texans answered the call to arms. They marched off to war, leaving their families at home to struggle with hostile Mexicans on the southern border and hostile Indians in the west.

After the Civil War ended in 1865, the Lone Star flag flew once more over an independent Texas republic. Texas did not become a state again until March 30, 1870.

Palmito Ranch near Brownsville was the scene of the last land battle of the Civil War.

The Twentieth Century

Texas began the twentieth century in grand style. In 1901, mining engineer A. F. Lucas struck oil at Spindletop. When the "gusher" shot into the air, it changed American industry. According to

The famous Spindletop gusher spewed thousands of gallons of oil into the sky before workers could cap the well.

geologist Michael T. Halbouty, Spindletop "started the liquid fuel age, which brought forth the automobile, the airplane, the network of highways . . . [and] untold comforts and conveniences."

When the United States entered World War I in 1917, the army found that the "wide open spaces" of Texas were ideal for training bases. Soldiers from all over the country came to Texas.

The most famous of all the facilities was Kelly Field. It was the first base for training men to fly the "newfangled" airplanes that would be "dogfighting" (an air battle between nearby fighter planes) in the skies of Europe. In World War II, the base grew. It trained a new generation of pilots for a new generation of military planes. Until Kelly Air Force Base closed on July 13, 2001, it was the oldest continuously operating flying base in the U.S. Air Force.

Texas became a national presence in politics by sending three Texans to the White House: Lyndon B. Johnson served from 1963 to 1969, George Bush from 1989 to 1993, and George W. Bush was elected in 2000. A fourth president, Dwight D. Eisenhower, was actually born in Texas, though he grew up in Kansas.

George Bush and George W. Bush were the second father and son to become president. First were John Adams (1797–1801) and John Quincy Adams (1825–1829).

In Texas as in other states, the civil rights movement was an important social advance. One landmark Texas case in 1950 opened the doors of the University of Texas law school to an African-American student. This happened four years before the Supreme Court case that produced an end to racial-segregation laws all over the country.

The struggle for civil rights continued through the twentieth century. Not only African Americans, but Mexican Americans and

Before the civil rights movement of the 1950s and 1960s, segregation was a part of life in Texas. Few African-American families could afford luxuries like this new touring car.

others made advances. As activist Thomas C. Rockeymoore put it, not only could African Americans sit in the front of the bus, "Nowadays, they can drive the bus."

Texans of all races are proud of their state's history. They look forward to the future, but they have not forgotten their history. They can't. The six countries who ruled Texas have become part of who they are.

"Colored only" signs were everywhere. There were a lot of places where we weren't allowed to try on clothes.

—Ethel Minor, remembering racial segregation in San Antonio, Texas

Important Dates

1519 Alonzo Alvarez de Pineda maps the Gulf coastline.

1598 Juan de Oñate plants the Spanish flag on Texas soil.

1682 The first permanent settlement is established near present-day El Paso.

1685 French explorer René Robert Cavelier, Sieur de La Salle lands on the Gulf coast.

1763 France loses its American possessions to England. Texas remains in Spanish hands.

1821 Mexico gains independence from Spain. The Mexican flag flies over Texas.

1836 The Texas Declaration of Independence is adopted.

1836 The thirteen-day siege of the Alamo begins on February 24. On April 21 Sam Houston defeats the Mexican army at San Jacinto.

1836 Texas becomes an independent republic.

1845 Texas becomes the twenty-eighth state.

Sam Houston

1846-1848 The Mexican War is fought.

1861-1865 The Civil War is fought. Texas joins the Confederacy.

1870 Texas rejoins the Union.

1876 The present state constitution is adopted.

1901 An oil discovery at Spindletop thrusts Texas into the petroleum age.

1930 Finding more oil near Turnertown marks the discovery of the huge East Texas Oil Field.

1962 NASA opens the Manned Spacecraft Center in Houston, later called the Johnson Space Center.

1963 Lyndon B. Johnson of Texas becomes president after the assassination of President John F. Kennedy.

1966 Barbara Jordan of Houston becomes the first African-American woman elected to the Texas Senate.

1989 George Bush of Houston becomes the forty-first president of the United States.

NASA Johnson Space Center

1990 Ann Richards becomes the first woman to be elected governor of Texas in her own right.

1994 George W. Bush is elected governor.

2000 George W. Bush is elected president of the United States.

3 The People

There is an old saying that Texas is not just a state of the Union; it is a state of mind. In other words, being from Texas is somehow special. A popular "Texas brag" puts it this way: "Never ask a man if he's from Texas. If he is, he'll tell you on his own. If he's not, no need to embarrass him."

Texans come from many different backgrounds. People of Native, Mexican, and African-American descent have helped to shape the state. Other cultures have also added to the mix, including Germans, Czechs, Irish, Italians, and Vietnamese. Many people outside Texas are unaware of this cultural variety. To them, Texas means one thing: cowboys.

Cowboy Ways

From the Dallas Cowboys of the National Football League to the fifty-two-foot-tall "Big Tex" statue at the state fairground, Texans love cowboys. The modern cowboy no longer has gunfights in the middle of a dusty Texas street or rides the Chisholm Trail—a cattle trail that led from Texas to Kansas—

Fun at the Texas State Fair

with a herd of longhorn cattle. He might be a cattle rancher with a college degree in livestock management. He might be a professional rodeo performer. He also might be an accountant or a computer programmer who likes to wear western boots and ten-gallon hats.

These modern "cowboys" may not ride horses or herd cattle. It does not matter. The legend of the tough-as-nails wrangler who lived by the code of the West is part of their heritage. Keeping it alive is a way of honoring the past.

Calf roping is a major event at every rodeo. The aim is to rope and tie the calf in the shortest time.

Mexican Americans

In the 2000 census, 32 percent of Texans claimed Hispanic origins. People of Mexican descent make up the largest Hispanic group in the state. They are concentrated in the south, near the Mexican border. Many live in poor neighborhoods called barrios, or colonias.

Good jobs are not easy to find in the barrio. Sooner or later, almost everyone who lives there works in the fields. Each year, migrant farmworkers go from farm to farm, following the harvest northward as far as Minnesota. The work is hard, and the wages are low.

Many south Texas towns maintain close relations with the Mexican towns just over the border. The border town of Eagle Pass proudly advertises itself as **"the place where YEE-HAH meets OLÉ."**

Each year, migrant farm workers pick thousands of acres of Texas cotton.

Making a Piñata

Many Mexican-American celebrations use a piñata (pin-YA-ta)—a hollow, candy-filled container shaped like an animal, cartoon character, or another design. You can make a piñata from newspaper and use it to play the piñata game.

What You Need

Plastic sheet or garbage bags to protect the table
Large balloon (non-helium)
Several sheets of aluminum foil or toilet-paper tubes
Masking tape (optional)
1 cup flour
2 cups water
Bowl and spoon
Several sections of newspaper
Pin
Several sheets of colored tissue paper
Scissors

White Glue
Hole punch
Wrapped candy
Three or four 12-inch pieces of dental floss
Strong cord
Blindfold
Broomstick or baseball bat

Cover up a table with plastic. This project is messy!

Blow up the balloon and knot it. If you like, shape the foil sheets or toilet-paper tubes into legs, a head, or other shapes, and tape them onto the balloon.

Mix the flour and water in the bowl, until it forms a paste.

Tear (don't cut) the newspapers into strips 1 to 2 inches wide. Dip a newspaper strip into the paste, slide the strip between two fingers to scrape off the excess paste, and wrap the strip around the balloon.

Repeat until you've covered most of the shape with three layers of over-lapping strips, with each layer running in different directions. Be sure to leave a 2-inch circular area uncovered on the top.

Let dry. This may take several days. Turn the balloon now and then so it dries on all sides. If the balloon hasn't popped, poke the pin through the uncovered area and pop it to form an opening.

Glue colored tissue paper everywhere except the opening. For a fluffier look, take strips of tissue paper and cut fringes along one side before gluing them on.

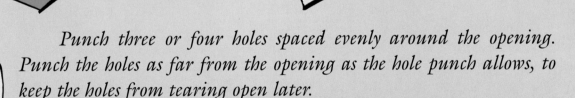

Punch three or four holes spaced evenly around the opening. Punch the holes as far from the opening as the hole punch allows, to keep the holes from tearing open later.

Put the candy in the opening. Thread a piece of dental floss through one of the holes and tie the ends together with a double knot, creating a loop. Repeat with the other holes. Thread the cord through all the loops and tie it with another double knot. Glue six or more lay-ers of tissue paper over the opening, one at a time, attaching them between the holes. Spread a thin layer of glue over each piece of tissue paper before attaching the next.

To play the piñata game, hang the cord over a tree branch or on a high hook. Take turns being blindfolded and swatting the piñata with a stick. When the piñata finally breaks, wait until the swatter removes the blindfold—then everyone dash for the candy!

The Ballet Folklorico de México always draws big crowds in Texas. Here, the troupe performs in Austin's Symphony Square.

Texas

Mexican Americans in Texas have created their own subculture. It is a blend of Mexico and Texas, known as Tejano (Tay-HAN-oh). The word, like the people it describes, is a blend of "Texan" and "*Méxicano.*"

Outside the Mexican-American community, Tejano culture is best known for its music. In the 1970s, singer Freddie Fender gave a Tejano flavor to hits like "Before the Next Teardrop Falls" and "Wasted Days and Wasted Nights." He sang in Spanish and in English, reaching a nationwide audience with music he described as Tex-Mex.

[Tejano music] is a combination . . . of a lot of different types of music all rolled into one package. It's country music, it's jazz, it has roots in the German polka, it also has Mexican music in it.

—Selena

Of course, not all Mexican Americans in Texas are famous singers or poor farmworkers. There is a growing middle class of Mexican Americans who practice medicine or law, own businesses, or work in government and high-paying technical jobs.

African Americans

The first African Americans in Texas came as slaves. After the Civil War, they worked to make a place for themselves as free people in a free society.

Until the beginning of the twentieth century, most blacks lived in the country. Many were sharecroppers. They rented the land that they farmed and paid the owner with a share of the crop.

Famous Texans

Red Adair: Firefighter

Houston-born Paul "Red" Adair is perhaps the most famous firefighter in the world. He specialized in putting out oil-well fires. These dangerous fires start deep in the earth, fueled by huge supplies of oil or natural gas. In 1962, Adair and his team put out a well fire in Algeria that had been burning for six months.

Lyndon B. Johnson: United States President

Lyndon B. Johnson, born near Stonewall, Texas, became president of the United States under terrible circumstances. He took the oath of office just hours after President John F. Kennedy was assassinated. Johnson completed Kennedy's term and won the presidency in the election of 1964.

Michael Johnson: Athlete

Runner Michael Johnson was born in Dallas. He made a habit of breaking world records and winning gold medals for track and field. In the 1996 Olympics, he won both the 200- and 400-meter races, becoming the first man in history to win gold in both events in the same Olympics.

Barbara Jordan:
Congressional Representative

In 1966, Barbara Jordan became the first African-American woman to be elected to the Texas senate. In a distinguished career, she went on to serve in the U.S. House of Representatives. When she died in 1996, she was buried at the Texas State Cemetery, an honor reserved for Texas heroes.

Selena Quintanilla Perez: Singer

Almost singlehandedly, the Texas singer known simply as Selena, put Tejano music on the map. She began performing in 1981 at the age of ten. At the Tejano Music Awards of 1987, she was named Female Vocalist of the Year and Performer of the Year. In 1991, her song "Ven Conmigo" became the best-selling Tejano record in history.

Gene Roddenberry:
Writer and Producer

In 1966, Gene Roddenberry launched a television series that would become an American legend: Star Trek. He created a believable future world with characters that came alive. Roddenberry received many honors, including three honorary doctorate degrees and a star on the Hollywood Walk of Fame.

Fifth graders from many different ethnic groups enjoy an Outdoor Education Camp in Bandera, Texas.

> *Earlier today, we heard the beginning of the preamble to the Constitution of the United States. "We the people." It is a very eloquent beginning. But when that document was completed on the 17th of September in 1787, I was not included in that "we the people." I felt somehow for many years that George Washington and Alexander Hamilton just left me out by mistake. But through the [democratic] process . . . I have finally been included in "we the people."*
>
> —Barbara Jordan, addressing Congress, July 25, 1974

In the mid-twentieth century, Texas had a population shift. People began leaving farms and rural towns for cities. Large numbers of African Americans joined in this move. Today, more than 40 percent of black Texans live in the urban areas of Dallas and Houston.

Houston's Fifth Ward is the largest African-American neighborhood in Texas. Many of the people who live there are poor, and there is street violence in the neighborhood. The school drop-out rate is high. In spite of this, the Fifth Ward has produced outstanding achievers, such as former heavyweight boxing champion George Foreman and Congressional Representatives George Thomas "Mickey" Leland and Barbara Jordan.

Native Americans

Dozens of Native American tribes once made Texas their home. Today, there are only three federally recognized tribal reservations in the state: the Alabama-Coushatta Reservation in the "big thicket" country of east Texas, the Tigua Community in the west, and the Kickapoo lands at Eagle Pass on the Mexican border.

The Alabama and Coushatta are two closely related tribes that share a reservation. They received their lands from Sam Houston himself, in 1854. It was his way of rewarding them for not fighting against the Texans during Texas's war with Mexico.

The Tigua of El Paso County are the last Pueblo Indians in Texas. *Pueblo* is the Spanish word for "town." Spanish explorers used it to refer to several southwestern tribes that lived in settled communities. The Texas Tiguas originally came from a pueblo in New Mexico, which was already well established when the Spanish first visited it in 1539. Though the Tigua have lived in west Texas since the 1670s, they were not officially called an Indian tribe until 1968.

The Kickapoo have roots on both sides of the Rio Grande. Their ancestral homeland lies in Mexico. Today, they live on a

Tigua dancers like this boy keep their ancient culture alive.

A song of the Tigua still remembers their ancient homeland:

My home over there,
Now I remember it,
And when I see it,
the mountain far away
Oh, then I weep,
Oh, what can I do?

reservation in southeast Texas. Kickapoo take pride in their heritage: "The tribe loves their language and all the traditions," said tribal chairman Raul Garza. "We want to keep it alive as long as we can. We don't ever want to lose it."

Other Texans

In the nineteenth century, many European immigrants settled in Texas. Today, some of their descendants enjoy keeping old-country traditions alive. For example, there is the German Singing Society in San Antonio and the Italian-American Cultural Society in El Paso. Every year, the Irish music festival draws big crowds to the state fairground in Dallas.

Texans of German heritage love celebrating their culture. Here, costumed children dance at the Wurstfest in New Braunfels.

Vietnamese-American students in Austin wear colorful costumes for a program celebrating Asian New Year.

People of Vietnamese descent are the newest Texans. After the Vietnam War ended in 1975, many refugees came to the United States. More than 52,000 chose to settle in Texas. They set up communities in cities like Dallas, Houston, and Austin, and along the Gulf coast.

Illegal Immigration: A Texas Issue

Each year, thousands of illegal immigrants come to Texas, mostly from Mexico. Most are desperately poor people who come seeking work. The cost of this illegal immigration runs into millions of dollars. For example, the Brownsville school district estimated that it spends $20 million per year to educate children who are in the country illegally.

The human cost is even higher. Illegal immigrants often live through nightmares getting to this country. Many pay smugglers, who bring them over in cruel conditions. In one case, the border patrol heard pounding from inside a truck they had just stopped. They found 113 people packed together inside. A little girl had passed out from lack of air.

Many unemployed Texans believe that illegal immigrants take jobs away from them. This can lead to resentment against all "foreigners."

> *[People] weren't exactly rude to me, but, when I used to work at the airport, we would have people . . . "throwing words," saying that these people come from another country to take their jobs, and why didn't they go back home. They didn't call my name, but I knew they meant me. . . . I didn't let it worry me because I'm legal here, so I didn't answer them.*
>
> —Alberto Brown, an immigrant from Panama

The government has tried to deal with the problem. The Federal Immigration Service has increased patrols along the border. Police are arresting smugglers and people who knowingly hire illegal workers. State and local governments are trying to deal with the money issues, while social-welfare agencies deal with the human ones.

Illegal immigration is just one of the social issues that Texans will have to handle in the twenty-first century. Bringing many different cultures together has never been easy. Minorities in Texas have had to deal with racial and ethnic prejudice. However, conditions are improving. People of Native, Hispanic, and African-American descent are gaining their rightful place in Texas society. The result is a richer life for all the people of the Lone Star State.

Calendar of Events

The Houston Livestock Show and Rodeo

Every February and March, the Houston Astrodome presents the largest stock show and second-largest rodeo in the nation. Young people from organizations such as the Future Farmers of America (FFA) come to show animals they have raised and compete for prizes. The rodeo features professional cowboys competing in traditional events such as bronco and bull riding, calf roping, steer wrestling, and barrel racing.

Fiesta San Antonio

Every April, this ten-day fiesta celebrates the battle of San Jacinto, which won the Texas war for independence in 1836. Events include parades, concerts, art exhibits, and fashion shows. In the evenings, downtown San Antonio comes alive with music and street dancing. The fiesta ends with a procession to the Alamo.

Cinco de Mayo

On May 5, 1810, four thousand Mexican troops won an unmistakable victory against a French army of eight thousand. It was the beginning of the end for the French colonial forces.

Today, Cinco de Mayo (sink-oh-duh-my-oh, Spanish for "fifth of May") fiestas celebrate that victory. The festival in Austin lasts four days, with music, pageants, and carnival rides. There is even a contest to see who can eat the most red-hot jalapeño (hal-ah-payn-yo) peppers.

Cinco de Mayo

Willie Nelson

Willie Nelson's Fourth of July Picnic

Thousands come to Luckenbach, Texas, to spend the Fourth of July weekend with country-music legend Willie Nelson. There's plenty of food and music in a laid-back atmosphere. Celebrities mingle with ordinary folks at this annual event.

The Bedford Blues Festival and Art Fair

Labor Day weekend is special for music lovers in Dallas. The Bedford Blues Festival and Art Fair comes to town. Visitors can watch a show at one of the outdoor stages, view artworks on display, and browse exhibits by local businesses.

The State Fair of Texas

October is state-fair time in Texas. The event is held on a 277-acre fairground outside of Dallas. It includes livestock exhibitions, football games, carnival rides, concerts, fireworks shows, and a grand parade. The Texas state fair is the largest in the nation, with over three million people attending every year.

Dickens on the Strand

On the first weekend in December, the Strand National Historic Landmark District in Galveston transforms itself into the Victorian London of author Charles Dickens. Dressed in costumes of the late 1800s, people gather to watch jugglers, magicians, acrobats, and dancers. Traditional folk-music groups perform on six stages throughout the district.

San Antonio is known for its beautiful mission architecture. This bell tower belongs to a church that is more than 250 years old.

4 How It Works

Texas is governed by the constitution of February 15, 1876. It became law six years after Texas rejoined the Union following the Civil War. Though it has been amended, or changed, many times, its basic form has stood the test of time.

Levels of Government

The state government deals with broad issues that affect all of Texas. It makes laws that everyone in the state must obey, and sets up guidelines in areas such as education, health care, and social welfare.

Many policies and programs are established at the state level and carried out by counties and cities. Texas has 254 counties, each governed by an official board known as a commissioners' court. Counties provide services ranging from schools and public hospitals to libraries, jails, and parks. A county sheriff is responsible for law enforcement.

I have always felt that one must give back to the community. Politics is one of the ways that I can do this.

—Mayor Elzie Odom, Arlington, Texas

An elected council, headed by a mayor, usually governs each city and town. In some cities, the mayor is the head of the

Branches of Government

The Texas state government has three branches: executive, legislative, and judicial. The governor is the chief executive of the state. The legislature makes its laws, and the courts enforce them.

Executive The governor is elected for a four-year term. He or she can call special sessions of the legislature, appoint members of boards and commissions, and veto (forbid) or approve proposed laws.

Legislative Like the U.S. Congress, the Texas legislature is divided into two houses— a senate and a house of representatives. The senate has 31 members, elected for four-year terms. The house has 150 members, who have two-year terms. Both houses must approve a bill before it goes to the governor for final action.

Judicial The judicial branch, or court system, enforces the laws of the state. The courts deal with two kinds of cases: criminal and civil. In a criminal case, someone is accused of a crime and can be sent to prison if convicted. Civil cases involve lawsuits in which one party seeks money from another. Examples of these are personal-injury cases or suits against a company for unfair business practices.

local government. In others, a professional city manager is hired to do this work.

Local officeholders may not be career politicians. Many have other jobs or are retired. For example, Mayor Grady Barr of Abilene is a roofing contractor. Mayor Elzie Odom of Arlington is a retired U.S. postal inspector.

The Texas capitol in Austin is an impressive sight under special lighting.

Bilingual Education: A Texas Issue

Texas lawmakers have struggled with bilingual education for years. In a state with such a large Spanish-speaking population, it is an important issue. At one time, Texas schools banned Spanish.

Students caught speaking Spanish were punished in different ways. In some schools, they had to pay a small fine each time they broke the "no Spanish" rule. In others, they were made to stand on a special black square or write "I must not speak Spanish" over and over again on the blackboard. In 1998, state Senator Carlos Truan could still remember the 1940s, when he was spanked for speaking Spanish in the playground.

Spanish was bad. It was forbidden.... You were punished if you spoke it . . . there were students in my elementary school that sometimes spoke the forbidden language. They had to pay a nickel or a dime, depending on the extent of the infraction [wrongdoing].
—Minerva Gorena, teacher

In 1973, the Bilingual Education and Training Act finally ended these policies. It required bilingual education in schools where twenty or more students in any one grade spoke limited English. School districts rushed to develop new programs. They had to find teachers who could teach mathematics, social studies, and science in Spanish. Standardized achievement tests had to be adapted for limited-English students.

Many Spanish-speaking students in Texas schools are fully bilingual.

How It Works

Making Laws in Texas

In 1997, a similar law dealt with adapting achievement tests for disabled students. Its progress through the legislature is a good example of the law-making process in Texas.

HB ("House Bill") 1800, as it was first called, came before the house of representatives on February 27, 1997. It was meant to give students in special-education classes a fair chance to show their skills. Most of the testing changes are a matter of common sense. For example, a blind student could not be expected to do well on tests that use visual directions and a deaf student could not be expected to do well on tests that involved listening.

On March 3, a summary of HB 1800 was read before the full house. It was then sent to the House Committee on Public Education for study. The committee went over it point by point, suggesting changes and asking questions. It held public hearings, which any interested citizen could attend.

When the study was completed, the committee sent the bill back to the full house. After more public readings and debate, the house passed HB 1800 and sent it to the senate. There it went through the same process of

Vietnamese-American students in Austin study English in ESL (English as a Second Language) classes.

readings, reports, and debates. On May 21, the senate passed the bill. On June 17, 1997, the governor signed HB 1800 into law.

By that time, this fairly simple bill had gone through forty-five different actions. If it had been more complicated or more controversial, the process would have taken even longer. There is a good reason for all this complexity. In Texas, as in other states, the procedure for passing a law includes a number of safeguards. They help to ensure the full and free debate that is the basis of the democratic process.

"Dear President Bush..."

Texas schools do their part to teach students about participating in government. An eighth-grade class at William B. Travis Middle School in Amarillo wrote letters to President George W. Bush as a homework assignment. Each student was supposed to tell the president about an issue that interested him or her. Alfredo Segovia chose education. In his letter he wrote, "Education is . . . a problem today. The dropout rate is on the rise. I don't use statistics. I see them. Everyday we see less and less students in schools. We also have a gang problem. Some schools are so used to these problems, that they think it is no big deal. This needs to end now!"

Like the lengthy process of lawmaking, citizen participation helps ensure that Texas government pays attention to the needs of the people. In any democracy that is the greatest goal of the political process.

Ordinary citizens of all ages can express their opinions to state and local officials. It is a good way to take part in the democratic process. The government encourages citizens of all ages to take part. There is even a Web site with information on how to contact every state official and agency in Texas: http://www.tsl.state.tx.us/trail/agencies.html

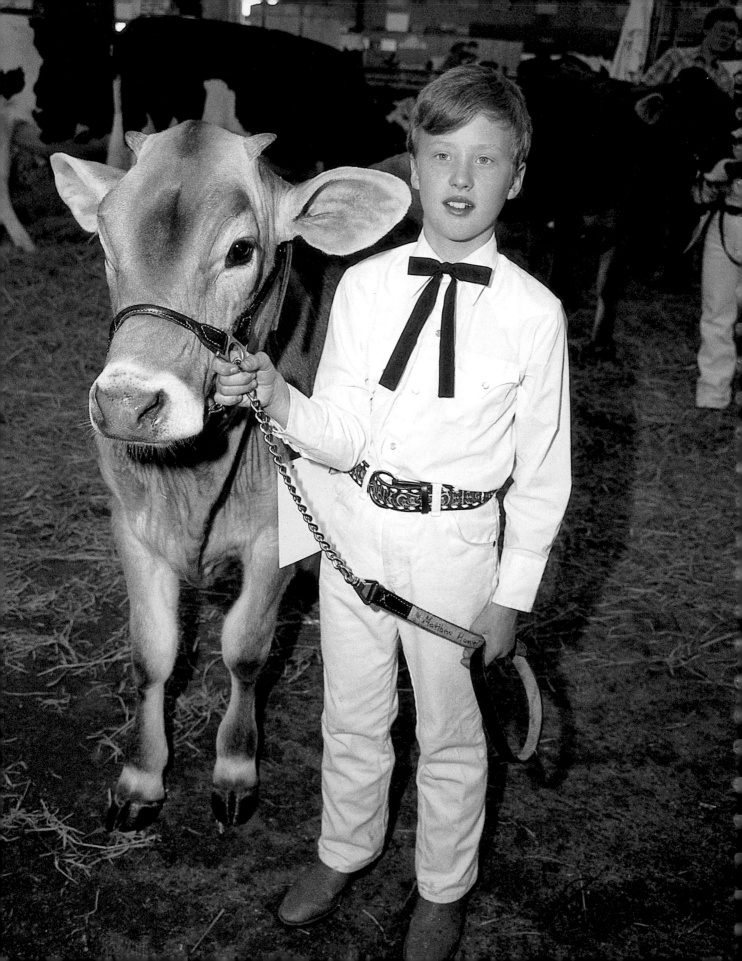

5 Making a Living

For many years, the Texas economy could be described in three words: cows, cotton, and crude (oil). From the vast cattle ranches of the west to the oil fields and forests of the east, Texans made a living from the state's abundant natural resources.

Today, the economy is more varied. Texas factories produce everything from children's clothes to vacuum cleaners and clock radios. Technology firms have turned Texas into a high-tech center rivaled only by California's famous Silicon Valley.

Agriculture

Texas produces a wealth of agricultural products. At the beginning of the twenty-first century, income from these products topped $13 billion. Cotton is the number one field crop, followed by sorghum grain, wheat, and corn. Other agricultural products include milk, eggs, cabbages, spinach, and watermelons. Texas also ranks among the five states that grow the most tree crops such as grapefruit, oranges, and pecans. It routinely leads the nation in raising cattle. Though cattle ranching is

At the San Antonio Livestock Exposition a boy prepares to show a cow he has raised.

A mechanical harvester harvests cotton near Thrall, in central Texas.

profitable, it is not easy. Drought and disease have always been enemies. For example, drought-related losses cost cattle ranchers over $329 million between September 1995 and May 1996.

Cotton is the largest cash crop in Texas. From the high plains to the blackland prairies, vast fields of fluffy white cotton "bolls" (pods) stretch across the landscape. One reason that cotton is so profitable is that almost every part of the plant is useful. The fiber becomes cloth, the seeds are used for cotton-seed oil, and the husks go into cattle feed.

Mining and Mineral Extraction

On January 10, 1901, a strange domed hill in southeastern Texas made history. Oil drillers had been working at Spindletop for weeks, with no results. That January morning did not begin well. Mud oozed up from the ground, filling the hole and getting in the way of the drill pipe.

Geologist Pete Nester explained what happened next: "After

a short time, the . . . workers set about to clean up the mess. . . . All of a sudden, a noise like a cannon shot came from the hole, and mud came shooting out of the ground like a rocket. Within a few seconds, natural gas, then oil followed . . . rising to a height of more than 150 feet. This was more oil than had ever been seen anywhere in the entire world."

The oil industry provides employment for thousands of Texans. This worker on an oil rig tends the machinery.

That was the beginning of another Texas industry—and another Texas legend. "Wildcatters," "roughnecks" and "oil barons" took their place beside cowboys. People loved to hear stories about wildcatters exploring for oil and roughnecks working in the fields. The wealth of the barons became its own legend. As one anonymous (unknown) Texan put it, these men were so rich they "could play Monopoly with real buildings."

An oil refinery in Port Arthur, Texas

Manufacturing

Texas manufacturing began with industries related to natural products: food-processing plants, textile (cloth) mills, and oil refineries. It expanded to include a wide variety of manufactured products.

In the 1990s, factory production decreased in industrial states such as Ohio, Pennsylvania, and New York. In Texas, it grew. By the end of the decade, Texas ranked second to California in the size of its manufacturing workforce.

High-Tech Texas

"High-tech" has come to stand for modern information and communication technologies. In a sense, the entire industry was born in Texas on September 12, 1958. On that day, electrical engineer Jack Kilby demonstrated his new invention: the microchip, or "integrated circuit." These tiny devices have made the computer and communications revolution possible.

Technology companies constantly work to improve old products and develop new ones. In 2000, Texas Instruments spent over $1.5 billion on research and development.

"The first circuits were very crude," said Kilby. "They would have perhaps . . . a dozen transistors. Today, our bigger chips have millions of transistors, so there's been a tremendous increase."

Kilby worked for what was then a medium-sized electronics company called Texas Instruments. Today, TI is a giant in the field, with over 35,400 employees worldwide. Jack Kilby has been hailed as a pioneer of the high-technology industries. In 1982, he became a member of the National Inventors Hall of Fame. In 2000, he was awarded the Nobel Prize for Physics.

Products & Resources

Cotton

Cotton is still king in Texas. About 6.3 million acres are planted each year.

Beef Cattle

Cattle ranching is not only a Texas tradition—it is a profitable business. In 1999, income from cattle production was $5.775 billion.

Timber

Timber represents over one-third of agricultural income in east Texas. Other sections of the state also profit from timber, through the manufacture of wood and paper products.

Wool and Mohair

Texas is a leading producer of wool, which comes from sheep; and mohair, which comes from angora goats. In 1997, the state produced 17.3 million pounds of wool and mohair at a value of $26.1 million.

Oil

Texas has the largest oil reserves in the nation. Its wells produce 1.2 million barrels of oil every day.

Technology

Texas and technology go together. In 2001, more than 400 thousand Texans were employed in high-tech industries.

The development of the microchip helped to transform Texas into a center of high-tech commerce. By 1995, technology industries employed more people than oil and gas and agriculture combined. In addition to a profitable business in the United States, Texas companies exported $29 billion worth of technology products, mostly to Mexico and Latin America.

Transportation

Transportation is critical in a state with vast areas of sparsely populated land. Texas has a network that includes cars, trucks, trains, planes, and ships. Over 71 thousand miles of state roads and 12 thousand miles of railroad tracks thread through the countryside. Four deep-water ports on the Gulf coast handle freighters carrying goods between Texas and foreign markets. There are airports for everything from single-engine crop dusters (they spread chemicals over fields from the air) to international jetliners.

Huge cargo ships transport Texas products to South America and other foreign ports.

Tourism and Recreation

In May 1998, Texas tourism officials came up with an unusual way to observe National Tourism Week. They wore bright green ribbons to work—green for the color of money. A Department of Economic Development employee explained

Thousands of tourists come every year to "remember the Alamo."

the ribbons with one sentence: "Texas tourism is something to celebrate." It is certainly profitable. By 1996, tourism had become the third-largest industry in Texas, topped only by real estate and oil and gas.

In 1998, Texas earned $34.6 billion from tourism, which created 370,000 jobs.

People come to Texas for many reasons. Some like the excitement of the cities. Others prefer lazing around on Gulf coast beaches. Families might spend a day or two at the Six Flags Over Texas amusement park near Dallas–Fort Worth or tour NASA's Lyndon B. Johnson Space Center in Houston.

Perhaps the most popular reason for vacationing in Texas is to experience the rugged country for which the state is famous. National and state parks preserve wilderness areas while making them available for people to enjoy.

The Big Thicket National Preserve is one of the strangest places in all Texas. In this dark, thick forest visitors can see everything from panthers and bobcats to carnivorous, or meat-eating, plants.

Protecting the Environment

Environmental protection is not limited to parklands and nature preserves. In Texas, taking care of the land is everybody's business. Endangered plants and animals must be protected. Air and water must be kept clean.

Protecting renewable resources is an important part of the environmental program. For example, responsible lumber companies plant as many trees as they cut down. This not only protects the forest habitat but provides a steady source of timber.

Renewable sources of energy, such as solar and wind power, are also important. Sunlight and wind are limitless and produce energy without polluting the air, water, or land. In

This strange plant is not growing on an alien planet. It is an agave in the Chisos Mountains of Big Bend National Park.

1999, the legislature passed a law requiring power companies to develop these resources.

Major government programs are not the whole story of environmental protection in Texas. Ordinary citizens also get involved. They recycle, volunteer for community cleanup days, and insulate their houses to use less energy.

Don't mess with Texas is the slogan of a statewide anti-litter campaign. TV ads have famous Texans spreading the word about cleaning up the highways and byways of the Lone Star State.

In the twenty-first century, Texans expect their state to grow and prosper. All the ingredients are in place. Government, business, and ordinary citizens are working together to protect the land. The economy is varied and prosperous. People of different racial, ethnic, and social groups are learning to live and work together. The result is a state that is proud of its past and confident of its future.

This flag was originally the flag of the Republic of Texas. The blue stripe stands for loyalty, the red stripe for bravery, and the white stripe for purity. It was adopted as the state's official flag when Texas became the twenty-eighth state in 1845. The state flag is called the Lone Star Flag and that is how Texas got its nickname.

The official state seal has a white star with five points and oak and olive branches tied together beneath it. Different versions of the seal had been in use throughout Texas's history, but in 1992 the secretary of state declared that this version would be the official design.

Texas, Our Texas

Words by Gladys Y. Marsh and William J. Marsh
Music by William J. Marsh

Tex - as, our Tex - as! all hail the might - y State!

Tex - as, our Tex - as! So won - der - ful and great!

Bold - est and grand - est, with - stand - ing ev - 'ry test; O,

Em - pire wide and glo - rious, You stand su - preme - ly blest.

God bless you, Tex - as! And keep you brave and strong, That

you may grow in power and worth, Thro' - out the a - ges long.

State Song

77

More About Texas

Books

Branch, Muriel Miller. *Juneteenth: Freedom Day*. New York: Cobblehill, 1998.

Burgan, Michael. *The Alamo (We the People)*. Mankato, MN: Compass Point Books, 2001.

Garza, Carmen Lomas. *Cuadros de Familia/Family Pictures*. San Francisco, CA: Children's Book Press, 1993.

Metz, Leon Claire. *Roadside History of Texas*. Missoula, MT: Mountain Press Publishing Company, 1995.

Stoecklein, David R. *The Texas Cowboys: Cowboys of the Lone Star State*. Ketchum, ID: Stoecklein Publishers, 1997.

Web sites

The Handbook of Texas Online:

http://www.tsha.utexas.edu/handbook/online/index.new.html

State of Texas Web site:

http://www.state.tx.us/

Texas State Historical Association:

http://www.tsha.utexas.edu/

About the Author

Linda Jacobs Altman has written many books for young people, including *Arkansas* and *California* in Benchmark Books' Celebrate the States series. She and her husband live in a small California town near a lake, with a house full of dogs, cats, and birds.

Index

Page numbers in **boldface** are illustrations.

FOLGER McKINSEY ELEMENTARY SCHOOL